## Bernie's Christmas Call

Copyright © SABGE Publishing 2021

All rights reserved. No part of this book should be reproduced without written consent from the publisher.

Names: Watermeyer, Sean, Author and Williams, Vanessa, Illustrator

Title: Bernie's Christmas Call by Sean Watermeyer

Description: Cardiff: SABGE Publishing [2021]

ISBN: 978-1-8380692-4-7

Subjects: Christmas, God, family

Manufactured in the UK

Written by Sean Watermeyer and Illustrated by Vanessa Williams

# Bernie's Christmas Call

Written by Sean Watermeyer

Illustrated by Vanessa Williams

On a Snowy Christmas Eve…………

The night was quiet when snowdrops fell,

from laden skies that night

And most were snuggled warm in their beds,

as the land was coated in white

The light from the street lamps fluttered, as

the snow descended down

All God's creatures sound asleep, in each

village, city and town

That same night Bernie the Christmas spirit, full of joy and Christmas love

Hitched a ride in Santa's sleigh, as it flew in starry skies above

Over hills and down into valleys, the reindeer pulled that sleigh

Bernie and Santa had lots of work, to make it a wonderful Christmas day

Now Santa's job was to drop off presents, for each little girl and boy

And Bernie's job was to sprinkle each house, with Christmas love and joy

So down each chimney both they went, with a squiggle and a squeeze

Laughing joyfully as they brushed against, the brightly-lit Christmas trees

And when Christmas Eve night was nearly done, every stocking filled to the top

And Bernie had left his Christmas spirit, in every home and every shop

It was then that Bernie and Santa stopped a while, to have a Christmas drink

And the reindeer scoffed down juicy carrots, with a smile and many a wink

Their work was done or so they thought, but huddled in one little house

T'was old Mrs Jones, her dog called Tom, and Harry a little brown mouse

The three of them sat and shivered, as the night went into the day

Cold and hungry old Mrs Jones, got on her knees to pray

"Dear God please help us this Christmas time, is there anyone to really care?
My dog Tom is cold Harry is hungry, and my wood cupboard is almost bare"
So God sent a message to Santa and Bernie, telling them of Mrs Jones plight
And Santa and Bernie gathered the Reindeer, and the sleigh once again took flight

It was early Christmas morning, when Santa's

sleigh reached her house

And Bernie and Santa were greeted joyfully, by

Tom and Harry, the mouse

It was then that Santa realised, all the presents in

his sleigh were gone

There was not even wood for Mrs Jones's fire, to

turn her heating on

So, Santa gathered his reindeer, and then carols they started to sing

And Bernie the spirit flew around the village, and the Church bells started to ring

In no time at all folk appeared, and the whole village came to life

And soon outside Mrs Jones house was every person, husband and wife

The villagers saw old Mrs Jones as she hobbled, out of her own front door

They could see she was cold and hungry, they could see she was lonely and poor

Then Bernie's spirit of love and kindness entered, each and every single heart

And every villager wanted to reach out and help, each to play their part

So wood was gathered for a roaring log fire, and a huge Turkey put on to roast

And Santa was invited for Christmas dinner, where he made a Christmas toast

The villagers all gathered around old Mrs Jones, as she sat in pride of place

And her loneliness just disappeared, and a smile came upon her face

The Reindeer were given carrots, and Harry a large piece of cheese

Tom was given an enormous bone and barked a thank you and please

Bernie smiled at all this kindness, of Christmas joy and fun

And he was content that this Christmas day, his work was finally done.

Merry Christmas!

If you liked this one, be sure to check out more Watermeyer & Williams books on Amazon!

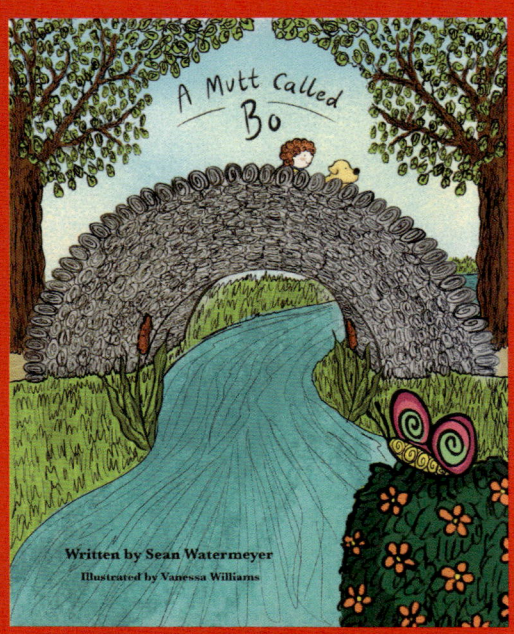

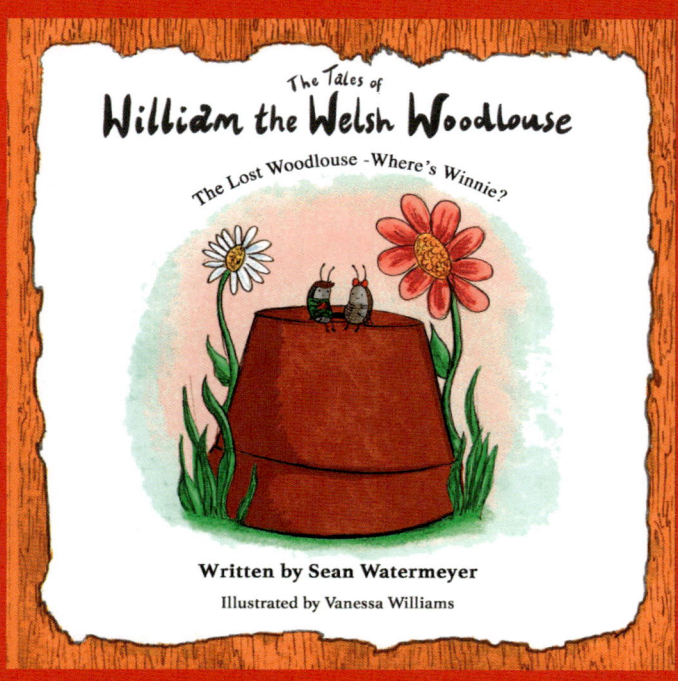

Printed in Great Britain
by Amazon